Sunset Ideas for
Bedroom &
Bath Storage

By the Editors of Sunset Books and Sunset Magazine

LANE PUBLISHING CO. • Menlo Park, California

We gratefully acknowledge the many architects, designers, and homeowners whose ideas have come together in this book. We also extend special thanks to Kathryn L. Arthurs, Hilary Hannon, and Marian May for their assistance in assembling the color section.

Editor, Sunset Books:
David E. Clark

First printing May 1982

Cover: A whole wall of closets distinguishes this handsome redwood bedroom. The section on the right includes a rod for hanging full-length garments; cubbyholes for sweaters and extra bedding; and a handy slanting shoe rack. To the left of the bathroom doorway are cubbyholes and a bank of drawers for shirts, lingerie, and other foldables; a tie rack; and a convenient dressing mirror. Further down the wall, double-decker rods (not shown) hold shorter garments.

The closet doors are louvered for ventilation; and to combat that closet pest, the moth, the closets feature cedar interiors. Architect: Donald Olsen. Interior design: Andrew Delfino. Photographed by Steve W. Marley. Cover designed by Zan Fox.

Supervising Editor:
Helen Sweetland

Staff Editor: **Susan Warton**

Contributing Editor: **Scott Atkinson**

Design: **Roger Flanagan**

Photo Editor: **JoAnn Masaoka Lewis**

Illustrations: **Joe Seney**

Mark Pechenik

Contents

Bedroom Storage

If you're concerned about making the most of space in your home, take a moment for this short quiz: Where do you watch Pavarotti at the Met? Where do you balance the family budget? Where do you iron? Where do your children play? Where do you accumulate those books you're planning to read? Where do you listen to your favorite record albums? And where do you enjoy a late-night snack?

Almost for sure, the answer to some or all of these questions is "in the bedroom." Because space is at a premium in most homes, bedrooms must perform a dual role—at least.

Take an inventory. Beyond the obvious bedroom basics, what extraneous items wind up in this room? How are you going to keep them easily usable, cared for, and housed in harmony with the bedroom decor? With a little ingenuity, you can organize supplies for hobbies, work, and precious moments of relaxation to keep your bedroom from becoming a center for uncontrolled clutter. Look at pages 16 and 17 for examples of well-organized double-duty bedrooms.

Children's rooms that double as play areas are shown on pages 24 and 25.

Looking at your bedroom with fresh eyes? Consider the largest space-gobbler of all—the bed. There's no real need for a bed to take up valuable space in today's small-scale bedrooms. If your ceiling is high, how about raising the bed off the floor? Sleeping lofts uncork gallons of space below for whatever activity you choose; we show some on pages 28 and 29. Or you may be interested in more down-to-earth ideas, such as the space-saving hide-away beds shown on pages 14 and 15.

When your bed must occupy a position of importance in the room, make it serve as a major storage spot. If you explore custom designs, you'll discover clever ways to tuck things around and under the bed. The headboard end of the bed offers plenty of storage potential too. Some attractive and practical storage headboards appear on pages 10 and 11, and bedside and underbed storage on pages 6 through 9. Included in this section is the ultimate bedside system, offering headboard, nightstand, bolster bins, and foot-of-the-bed storage.

You certainly won't have to sacrifice storage if you choose to use the head of your bed as a room divider—take a look at the dual-purpose headboards on pages 12 and 13.

When it comes time to rest, you'll want to surround yourself with amenities. Do you need to lodge (and possibly conceal or camouflage) bulky equipment for musical or televised entertainment? You'll find ideas on pages 18 through 23.

What about nighttime reading? Are a couple of shelves adequate—or will you need a wall-length bookcase, as shown on page 18?

On pages 26 and 27 you'll find ideas for accommodating such bedtime comforts as extra pillows and quilts—items too bulky to reside easily in the average linen closet or bureau. Instead, pouf them into a hollow headboard or under a convenient window seat.

What you need to store, of course, depends on how you live. The storage units or systems you choose are a matter of taste and budget. You may be among the people who like the relatively informal, open look of simple bins or baskets—sometimes the things we need to store look pretty enough to display at the same time. Or you may prefer to shut away most of your possessions behind closed drawers, doors, or draperies. In either case, efficiency should be a common denominator.

Happily, reorganizing bedroom space doesn't necessarily require that you hire a contractor, or even a carpenter. This chapter offers many ideas you can use even if your carpentry skills are limited (the *Sunset* book *Basic Carpentry Illustrated* might be just what you need). Or you can take your suggestions to a cabinetmaker or designer for the ultimate in individualized storage.

Whatever your storage requirements, whatever your taste, you'll find a bounty of good ideas to stimulate your thinking as you leaf through the forthcoming chapter.

A Bedside Storage System

Four easy-to-build units that you can use separately
—or in various combinations—to boost bedside storage

Build just one component—or build them all

A small bedroom, especially one that doubles as a home office or den, is a storage challenge. One way to maximize bedroom space is to make the bed itself (a space-waster for two-thirds of the day) as storage-efficient as possible.

The system shown here almost frames your mattress with places to stow things. Since you may not need this much storage at once, the four pieces—a headboard, a nightstand, a bolster with bins, and a foot-of-the-bed chest—are designed to work independently, as well as in various combinations. Just choose what fits your storage needs, your room layout, and your taste; alter the suggested dimensions as you wish. The four components are described in detail below and on the facing page.

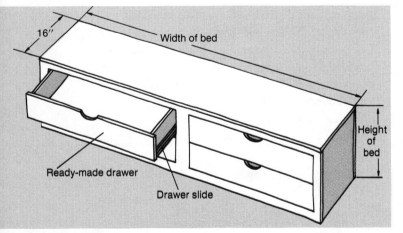

16″
Width of bed
Ready-made drawer
Drawer slide
Height of bed

The foot-of-the-bed chest

A low chest of drawers at the foot of a full-size bed has nearly the same storage capacity as a traditional bedroom bureau, yet it's not nearly as bulky. It can also double as a bench or television shelf.

You can buy a unit built especially for the foot of the bed; or try one designed for a different purpose (such as storing engineers' maps and blueprints).

To put together a chest like the one shown, build a frame from ¾-inch plywood, then install four ready-made drawers on standard slides. Make the chests the same height and width as your bed and approximately 16 inches deep.

Another foot-of-the-bed chest appears on page 26.

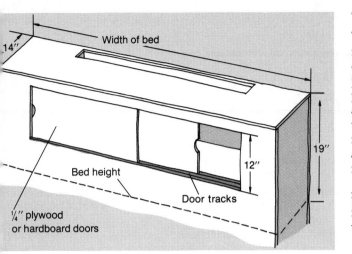

The headboard

This simple yet handsome unit has a storage compartment with handy sliding doors to hide clutter. Its flat top offers a useful surface with an inset at the back that's just deep enough to display magazines and books. The portion of the headboard above the mattress should be approximately 19 inches high and 14 inches deep; the width and overall height of the headboard will be determined by the size of your bed. Sheets, blankets, quilts, and bedspreads alter measurements, so it's wise to measure when these are in place.

Build the headboard from ¾-inch plywood. Use ¼-inch plywood or hardboard for the sliding doors, and install plastic, wood, or metal door tracks. Finish the unit with enamel.

You'll find another easy-to-build headboard on page 27.

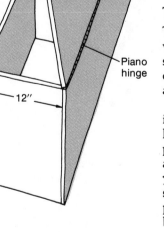

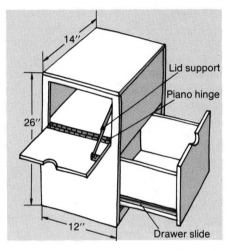

The nightstand

Two storage compartments are stacked inside this compact unit. The top one is a cubbyhole with a hinged, drop-down door in front; below it is a roomy drawer that pulls out from the side.

The nightstand shown here is approximately 12 inches wide, 14 inches deep, and 26 inches high; you can adjust these dimensions to suit your own needs. (To use the nightstand alone, you'll probably want to make it both wider and deeper, with a bottom drawer that pulls out from the front.)

Build the unit from ¾-inch plywood. Buy a ready-made drawer—or build your own—and install it on standard drawer slides. Finish the nightstand with enamel.

The bolster bins

The padded lid of this bedside box hinges open to reveal storage bins for bedding, out-of-season clothing, sewing or sports equipment, or miscellaneous bedroom clutter. The whole assembly—bottom, sides, dividers, and lid—is made from ¾-inch plywood.

Build the box the same height as your bed (or a few inches shorter); box length will be determined by the length of your bed and by the arrangement of the other pieces in your bedside storage system. Twelve inches is a convenient width for the unit, making it unobtrusive, yet wide enough so the bolster can double as a dressing seat or midnight-snack counter. Attach the lid with a piano hinge, and cover all the exposed surfaces of the box (or just the lid) with carpet or foam-backed fabric.

Use bolster bins on one, two, or all four sides of your bed.

Underbed Storage

If the area under your bed collects nothing but dust, add chests or pull-outs—or a custom-designed storage platform—to utilize that wealth of wasted space

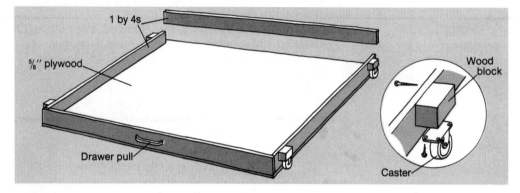

Make your own roll-out drawers

Even a standard metal bedframe can accommodate underbed storage. Add casters (remembering to allow an inch or so for clearance—more for thick carpeting) to ready-made shallow drawers—or to ones that you build yourself.

To construct a simple underbed drawer, fasten strips of 1 by 4s around the edges of a ⅝-inch plywood bottom (as shown), then add the wood blocks and casters, and attach a handle. A plywood lid will keep stored items free of dust—but you'll have to either pull the drawer out completely for access, or hinge the lid in the center.

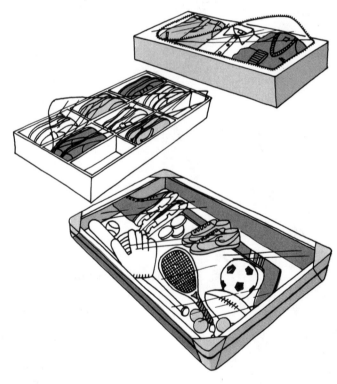

Custom bed holds roll-around cart

Designing a new bed? Consider leaving space for a handy roll-around cart with storage compartments, like the one shown here. Tucked away, the unit blends in with the rest of the underbed cabinetry. Pulled out, the cart doubles as a nightstand or breakfast-in-bed table.

Ready-made containers slide under standard bedframes

Trays and chests made expressly for underbed storage are commercially available in plastic, wood, and cardboard. Many have dividers; most have lids or see-through vinyl covers. These inexpensive storage aids are perfect for shoes, out-of-season clothing, bed linens. Look for them in the notions sections of department stores, or in mail-order catalogs.

Cabinetry creates base for platform bed

This 120-square-foot guest bedroom/office boasts more storage space than many bedrooms twice its size— thanks to a handsome platform bed with banks of drawers and a cabinet built in. Guests climb up to the sleeping level on three steps which are incorporated into the adjoining desk. Architect: Violeta Autumn.

Bedframe features double-decker drawers

Two levels of drawers are built into this striking bed-frame, which is coated with glossy black lacquer. The upper level is perfect for sweaters and lingerie; the lower level is roomy enough for extra bedding. Heavy-duty metal slides let the drawers open and close smoothly. Architect: Wendell Lovett. Interior design: Suzanne Braddock.

Headboard Storage

The head of a bed can do much more than prop up pillows

Bed-hugging headboard

Warm wood cabinetry wraps comfortingly around the head of this bed. Long and sleek, yet somehow snug in appearance, the sweeping headboard furnishes individual niches for a number of bedside conveniences. It even houses a stereo system, a luxury far too cumbersome for most headboards to accommodate. Just behind the slanting backrest, three hatches keep a telephone (its jangle muffled) and extra bedding hidden from view but easy to reach. Design: Richard Pennington.

Headboard appropriates a whole wall

Commodious and versatile, this headboard wall system provides generous storage for everything from books to clothing to Christmas tree lights, while catering to bedside needs. Tucked into its custom-fitted alcove, the head of the bed has behind-the-pillows storage and a ledge for midnight snacks. For reading, there's ample light from the recessed fixtures above. Design: Eurodesign Modular Furniture.

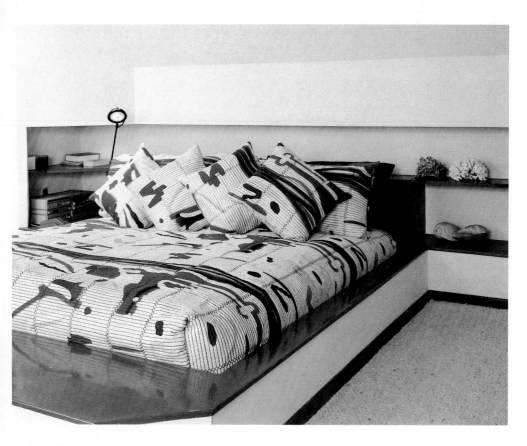

Polished wood for a shipshape sleeping alcove

This handsome platform bed sports a wraparound deck of glossy mahogany. Extending from the deck at the head of the bed are a slanted backrest/headboard with a flip-open top for storage, and open shelves that carry as much or as little bedside paraphernalia as the owners wish, from audio equipment to seashells. Design: MLA/Architects.

Open-and-shut case for bedside storage

Flap-door bins at the head of this bed hide bulky items such as spare linens and pillows. Closed, the doors double as a slanting backrest. (For safety, the doors are never left open when the bed is occupied.)

The compartment on the left houses provisions for nighttime comfort and security: an intercom and light controls for the entire house. Drawers on each side of the bed provide additional storage. Design: Ron Yeo.

Room-dividing Headboards

A two-faced approach to both spatial and storage needs

Floating island in a tranquil setting

In this pretty, pale bedroom, the bed takes center stage—it's a serene island of comfort as well as hard-working storage. Its massive yet sleek headboard is the focal point, partitioning the room into sleeping and dressing areas. On the sleeping side, almost hidden behind the bed pillows, cabinet doors cover storage crannies for bedside necessities; above them, an airy alcove more than accommodates reading lamps, books, a clock-radio, and a pretty plant. On the opposite side, the headboard serves up a dozen drawers, topped with a mirrored niche for toiletries and a jewelry box. Architect: Phoebe T. Wall.

Extra warmth on one side, extra storage on the other

In a bedroom of generous size, this freestanding fireplace wall separates a cozy sitting area from the sleeping quarters. On the headboard side of the wall, bookshelves surround a center panel that offers swing-arm lamps—and plenty of space to prop pillows—for bedtime reading. Architects: The Bumgardner Architects.

Handsome, clever, and capacious

More than compensating for the bedroom's single small closet, this vast bedframe-headboard-wardrobe unit also creates a private dressing corridor behind the bed. In front, tawny oak shelves climb nearly to the ceiling, framing an upholstered backrest. In back, the same rich oak forms a capacious set of cabinets and drawers. Design: The Butt Joint.

Hideaway Beds

For small bedrooms, guest bedrooms, double-duty bedrooms—
sleeping facilities that literally come out of the woodwork

Sleepy? Just pull down the wall

Mr. Murphy's popular patented invention of 1905 tilted out of a closet. Today's streamlined versions operate in similar fashion, concealing themselves during the day behind a door or a "secret panel," like the one shown here. The homeowners just pull on the painting's frame, and down comes a full-size platform bed—a readymade, commercially available unit that was incorporated into a new wall during remodeling. Architects: The Burke Associates.

Daytime seating becomes nighttime bedding

Nestled in a nook of a none-too-spacious cedar cabin, the built-in bench pictured above gets in nobody's way during the day. And when it's bedtime, the base and cushion fold out separately, transforming the seating area into the double bed shown on the left. Separate supports for the sleeping platform are kept in a drawer beneath the bench during the day. Architects: Larsen, Lagerquist & Morris.

Double-duty Bedrooms

Managing the paraphernalia when sleeping quarters
share space with hobbies or homework

In the mode of yesteryear

Dressmaking is one of those hobbies that are notorious for clutter. Yet neatness really counts when you're thick in the folds of a complicated project. In this sewing corner, functional antiques and a home-designed wall cabinet handle quantities of dressmaking supplies without disturbing the old-fashioned look of the bedroom.

On the left, thread spools parade their colors in a turn-of-the-century display case. The lace-bedecked figure above it is a child-size Victorian dress form. These days an electric machine stands on the antique treadle cabinet. Above it, the sewing notions sit in small drawers made from aluminum bread pans faced with wood.

Corner cutout for paperwork in privacy

For book-balancing or tax forms, thank-you notes or PTA flyers, epic poems or crossword puzzles, a small home office certainly aids achievement. But where to put it? Most homes nowadays lack spare rooms that aren't already reserved for the television or visiting relatives.

As this situation shows, a bedroom corner may provide the ideal location—out of traffic's way and relatively private. This office is neatly tucked into an alcove originally intended as a closet. The angles of the desk allow for leg room and a bank of drawers, as well as vertical slots large enough for sketch pads and blueprints; the wrap-around desktop offers ample work space. Overhead, a small bookcase completes the corner. Architect: David Jeremiah Hurley. Interior design: Jois.

Camera cache in a closet

Most of us connect closets with clothing. Naturalists may think first of moths, psychiatrists and genealogists of skeletons. But to an enthusiastic photographer, the closet in a spare bedroom can serve quite a different purpose: safely storing all the delicate and valuable apparatus of his craft. Here, floor-to-ceiling adjustable shelves behind bifold closet doors keep cameras and gear in tidy, easily accessible order. There's even room on the closet floor for a small refrigerator for film. Closet interior: Just Closets.

Bedroom Wall Systems

Cabinets, drawers, open shelves keep your private world in order

Bedroom bibliotheque

At the end of a weary day, some of us hit the hay, some of us hit the sack, and some of us also hit the books, at least for a little while before we doze off. For inveterate bedtime readers, bookshelves figure significantly in bedroom storage arrangements. Here, an orderly and cheery wallful of literature offers abundant possibilities for collecting, rearranging, perusing, lending, borrowing, displaying and, of course, reading. Architects: Rachlin Architects.

Wall-length whatnot

What, exactly, a whatnot holds is entirely up to its owner's fancy. While this one is less ornate and more purely functional than what Grandma might have called a whatnot, it certainly has all the versatility of those nostalgic storage pieces. Like the cabinetry shown on pages 20 and 21, it houses a television, as well as books and clothing, and then extends itself into a dainty glass-topped writing desk. Architects: Woody Dike and Tom Moore. Cabinet design: L. W. Grady.

That's entertainment!

On display here are some of the essentials of a bedroom entertainment center: stereo components, a library of record albums, and several shelves of books. For stow-away storage, this attractive wooden wall system also offers drawers and more drawers, cabinets and more cabinets. Three cubbyholes along the countertop have the same kind of covering found on roll-top desks. For ideas on storing the bedroom TV—another entertainment essential—turn to pages 20 and 21. Architect: Robert C. Peterson.

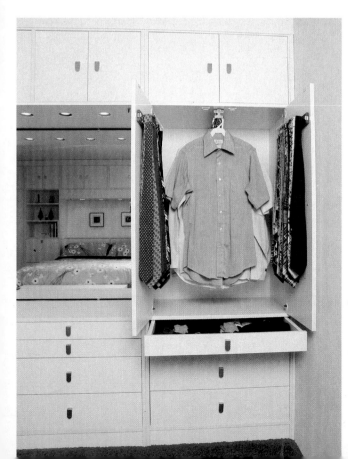

In a nutshell—it's natty

Open the big doors in this wall unit, and what do you find but a handy small-scale closet. Crisp shirts on a pullout rod line up along its center, while neckties hang neatly from racks placed high on either cabinet door. With nary an inch of wall space wasted, cabinets and drawers abound, surrounding the counter and recessed mirror. Design: Eurodesign Modular Furniture.

Television Storage

Keeping the set out of sight when it's out of mind

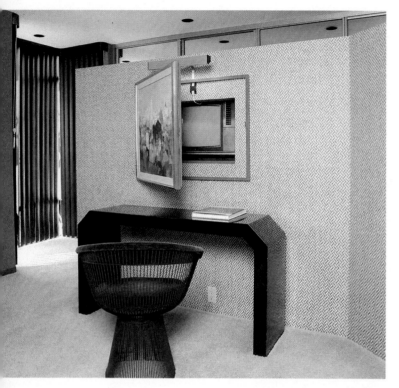

Artful camouflage

A framed painting swings back against the wall, allowing this television set to retire modestly from view when nobody's watching it. Without intruding on the sleek bedroom decor, the set is still ready for action when Bogart wakes up the wee hours of the TV schedule. Architect: William W. Hedley, Jr. Interior design: Charles Falls.

Sharing space with the shirts

The owner of this handsome, custom-built armoire can watch the morning news as he selects a shirt for the day. The television is bolted securely to a swivel-topped pull-out shelf, so it can be turned or brought forward for easier viewing. But when TV time is over, and the armoire doors are closed, there's no hint of the screen—or the shirts.

Even in antique storage pieces, there are often nooks and crannies that can be used for television storage; two antique hideaways are shown on pages 22 and 23. Interior design: Anona Colvin.

Cornering a super screen

For people who like wide video horizons, projection television has become a popular new luxury in home entertainment. But what about those times when you'd like it to be out of sight and out of mind? One simple solution, decoratively effected here, is to place the whole works in a vacant corner, then hide it all behind tall bifold doors. Interior design: Curt Graham.

Now you see it, now you don't

In a little hole-in-the-wall of its own, this television nestles discreetly under the sill of a greenhouse window. Cabinet doors shut it away from view when it's not being used. The drawer below and the narrow cabinets on either side provide additional bedroom storage. Architects: Ted Tanaka and Frank Purtill.

Antique Storage Furniture

Yesterday's chests and dressers still hold their own as storage units

From the Far East—a *chan jang*

Originally a Korean kitchen cupboard, this good-looking antique now accommodates the needs of a Western bedroom. A unique catch-all, it neatly tucks away shoes, handbags, sweaters, sewing paraphernalia, books, and even a tiny television set.

Crafted in the 19th century of elm wood, the wonderfully mellowed piece has been lined with pages of calligraphy from an old Korean book. Small drawers at the top serve handily for such items as jewelry, scarves, or billets-doux. *Chan jang* courtesy of Sloan Miyasato.

A bit of old Peking, by way of Europe

During the late 19th century period that we usually associate with Art Nouveau, French aristocrats took a liking to the exotic yet rustic look of Chinese furnishings designed at the time expressly for export to Europe. This dresser, of burnt bamboo and woven cane, may once have graced a fashionable country boudoir in the south of France. Today its deep drawers hold a multitude of 20th century foldables. Interior design: Ruth Soforenko Interiors.

Victorian hideaway for books, TV

Last century's clothes-keepers can be refurbished to suit contemporary tastes and to hold one of this century's most popular inventions. This richly carved Victorian armoire, American-made of oak, was stripped, bleached, and finally waxed to show off its natural golden color. The interior has been lined, and the doors upholstered, in a fabric that matches the bedroom wallpaper. Finally, a swivel-topped, pull-out plywood tray was added to hold a television set. Interior design: Ruth Soforenko Interiors.

Eastlake's "plain" is modern-day fancy

True to the dictates of Charles Eastlake's *Hints on Household Taste,* published in 1872, this charming dresser of the "golden oak" era looks almost austere for a Victorian piece. But its simple ornamentation (carved rather than superficially stamped into the solid wood) and pretty round mirror lend eye-catching style to this present-day bedroom.

Children's Rooms

Storing toys so they're easy to reach,
easy to put away, and easy on the eyes

Tomato-tone lockers for play area

Playtime paraphernalia can be stashed in metal lockers
just like the ones used in schools and gymnasiums. (To
find dealers in your area, look under "Lockers" in the
Yellow Pages of your telephone directory.) Sandwiched
between the lockers are baskets of vinyl-coated wire for
visible storage; they slide in and out on their own
heavy-duty plastic framework. A butcher block countertop ties the system together and provides additional
storage space. The cork bulletin board above displays
posters and drawings—and keeps the walls free of tacks
and tape. Interior design: Joan Simon.

Bunkbeds with built-in storage bunkers

An expansive drawer slides out from beneath these
clean white plastic laminate bunkbeds to deliver toys to
the adjacent play area. At the end of the beds is a mini-
armoire with adjustable shelves for clothing, as shown
here, or for additional toys. The cabinet top doubles as a
nightstand for the upper bunk. Furniture courtesy of
Julianus Associates.

The building blocks of a toy storage system

Versatile storage modules do more than organize mountains of playthings. They can be combined to form desks, platform beds, room dividers, and wall systems—then rearranged to suit the changing needs of growing children. You can buy ready-made modules in wood, particle board, or plastic—or you can build your own.

Construct your modules from ¾-inch plywood suitable for painting. A convenient size for each module is 16 inches square; for compatibility, make rectangular ones 16 by 16 by 32 inches. Add shelves (they double as vertical dividers when you rearrange the modules), hinged doors, even simple drawers; use wood molding or veneer tape to hide the plywood edges. Finish the modules with enamel—a single bright shade or a rainbow of colors.

If you stack several modules, be sure to bolt them to the wall or floor—or to each other—for stability.

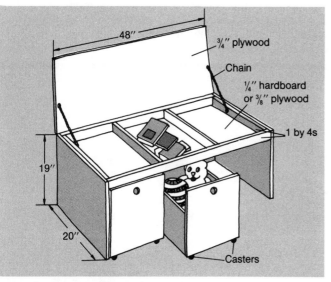

Drawing desk holds
a row of rolling toy bins

With the lid down, a toy bin or two pulled out, and a small chair pulled up, this handy unit serves as a drawing desk. But when playtime is over, the toy bins slide under the desktop to form a single, compact storage unit. Desk sides and lid are built from ¾-inch plywood; the bottom of the divided tray is made of ⅜-inch plywood or ¼-inch hardboard; and the tray frame is built from fir 1 by 4s. The unit illustrated is 19 inches high, 20 inches deep, and 48 inches wide, but you can adjust these dimensions to suit your child's needs.

Assemble the desk with glue and woodscrews or finishing nails. Attach the swing-up lid with a piano hinge, and add a lid support (or chain) at each end. Depending on the dimensions of your unit, the drawers of an old file cabinet might furnish ready-to-use bins (just add casters); or make your own bins from plywood. Finish the desk and bins with bright-colored enamel.

Stuffed animals
on display

A doll tree can store a whole crowd of cuddly companions. Made from a closet rod 1⅜ inches in diameter, the tree stands in a Christmas-tree holder which has been bolted to the floor for extra stability. To attach the dolls, sew small plastic rings to their backs, and hang them from cuphooks screwed into the "trunk" of the tree.

Oversize Storage

If bulky items are a king-size storage problem,
try one of these large-capacity solutions

Capacious compartments under seat cushions

Window seats aren't merely delightful places to curl up with a novel and a mug of coffee. Below those comfortable cushions are jumbo-capacity drawers, pull-out bins, or simply a large enclosed space that's reached through a hinged top or cabinet doors.

Window seats are basically either "built-in" or "built-out." The first type is usually built into a window alcove during construction or a major remodeling. The second type, which can be added on later, is essentially a long, narrow cabinet that's built out from the wall below an existing window. You can extend a built-out window seat along an entire wall—or around a whole room. Or, to achieve a built-in effect, you can install a wall system on both sides of a window, and build a seat in the "recess" created below the window.

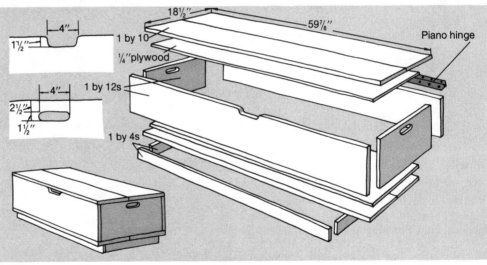

Get a firm foothold on oversize storage

There are scores of chests commercially available that can handle foot-of-the-bed storage—from steamer trunks and footlockers to rattan hampers and handsome cedar chests. But it's easy—and inexpensive—to build one of your own.

With a cushion on top, this clear pine storage chest doubles as a dressing seat. The four sides are cut from 1 by 12s; the lid and bottom are each made from two side-by-side 1 by 10s backed with one piece of ¼-inch plywood (the plywood pieces are cut slightly smaller—17 by 58⅜ inches for the chest illustrated here—to slip between the 1 by 12 frame); and the entire unit rests on a base made from 1 by 4 strips. The dimensions shown are for a queen-size chest, but you can adjust them to fit your own bed.

For another foot-of-the-bed idea, see page 6.

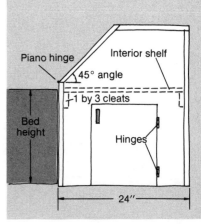

Easy-to-build hollow headboard

With two storage levels, this good-looking headboard has plenty of room for bulky items such as pillows and comforters. What's more, the door of the upper compartment doubles as a slanting backrest.

The depth of the unit is 24 inches. Make the headboard 12 inches taller than your bed and 2 inches wider. The backrest/door slants back at a 45-degree angle just above mattress level.

Build the headboard from ¾-inch plywood. Before assembly, cut a door out of each side piece (for access to the lower compartment). Assemble the pieces, nail 1 by 3 cleats to the inside of the headboard to hold the interior shelf, and attach the backrest/door with a piano hinge. Reattach the side-piece doors with hinges, and add door pulls and magnetic catches. Finish the headboard with enamel.

For another easy-to-build headboard and more bedside storage ideas, see page 7.

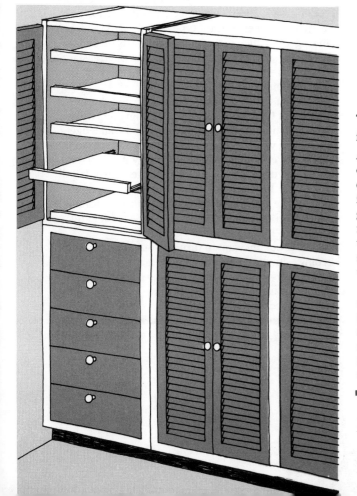

Towering pillar for paraphernalia

A floor-to-ceiling storage column offers space enough for everything from sweaters and lingerie to extra blankets. It might be part of a larger wall system, or it can stand alone in an otherwise unused corner.

Ready-made storage columns are available in furniture showrooms and home centers. You can also have a cabinet-maker design a unit to fit your special needs.

Sleeping Lofts

If your bedroom has a high ceiling, elevate your sleeping area
to open up storage or living space below

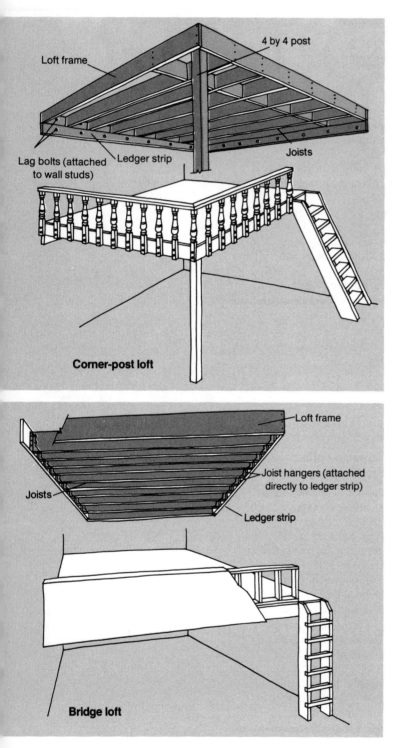

Corner-post loft

Loft frame

4 by 4 post

Ledger strip

Joists

Lag bolts (attached
to wall studs)

Loft frame

Joist hangers (attached
directly to ledger strip)

Joists

Ledger strip

Bridge loft

Lofty ideas

Lofts are simply elevated platforms that add floor space
—and visual interest—to a room. They're especially useful in studio apartments (renters should check with the
landlord before building, of course) and in bedrooms
that double as work or entertainment centers.

Ceiling height, obviously, is a critical factor. As a
practical guide, consider 6½ feet the minimum headroom needed for standing below a loft, and 4½ feet the
minimum headroom needed for sitting up in the bed
above. (But always check your local building codes; the
requirements for your area may be different.) Add
another foot for the structure of the loft itself, and you'll
find that you need a ceiling that's about 12 feet high. If
you have the 8-foot ceilings that are standard in so
many newer homes, you'll have to remove all or part of
the existing ceiling, or be content with the more "down-
to-earth" forms of underbed storage (see pages 8–9).

Two basic loft designs are illustrated here. The corner-
post loft is supported by a ledger strip on one wall and
two corner posts, or by ledger strips on two adjoining
walls and one corner post. The bridge loft touches three
adjoining walls and is supported by ledger strips on the
two opposing ones. A third type (not shown) is a freestanding loft, which requires support posts on all four
corners with braces to prevent sway. But the freestanding
loft is not as sturdy as the other two, and it's more complicated to build.

Once you've determined your design and dimensions, check them with your local building department.

Use structural fir for the loft frame and wall ledgers.
(Essentially, you're building a new floor and supporting
it above the existing one, so the size of your structural
lumber will depend on the number of feet the loft will
span. Check local codes.) You'll also need ¾-inch plywood for the loft floor, 4 by 4s of structural fir for any
corner support posts, and materials for a ladder and
safety rails.

You'll probably want to furnish your loft simply, in
keeping with its small scale. And remember that it's a
sleeping loft—not designed for heavy storage.

Some ideas for using the new space *under* your loft
are illustrated on the facing page.

Mini-library

Need a peaceful retreat for reading or listening to music? Create a cozy den below your sleeping loft by adding shelves for books, records, and stereo components. If you have a bridge loft (see facing page), just fasten shelves to the walls underneath it using L-braces or adjustable tracks and brackets. With a corner-post loft, let the backs of freestanding bookcases define the walls of your new mini-library. For comfort, add your favorite chair, an area rug, and a good reading lamp.

Office or sewing room

Turn your underloft space into a compact office by setting up a desk or drawing table, bookshelves for reference books and supplies, a telephone, and a file cabinet. Or create a sewing room by installing a sewing machine, a counter for cutting out material, drawers for fabric and patterns, a wall organizer for thread and notions, and perhaps a pull-out ironing board. If you have a bridge loft—or if you've added walls beneath your corner-post loft—you can hang cabinets or shelves from the wall studs and not encroach on precious floor space.

Walk-in closet & dressing room

Install a closet rod or two beneath your loft, then add a bank of drawers and a dressing table with a lighted make-up mirror, and you've created a walk-in closet that doubles as a dressing room. Sliding or folding louvered doors will keep the area private yet well ventilated. For more closet and dressing-room ideas, see the next chapter, pages 30–53.

Closets & Dressing Areas

Many of us, preoccupied with our busy lives, turn a negligent eye to the state of our closets until the calendar announces the season for old-fashioned spring cleaning. And sometimes even that isn't enough to nudge us.

At the same time, just about everyone would really like to have a nice, orderly closet—a closet so well planned and tidy that a beloved garment could be easily found, and in sparkling condition, rather than crumpled from crowding. Though they may seem insignificant in the larger context of life, the small details of what we wear actually have quite a resounding effect on how we feel about ourselves throughout each day. In the upcoming chapter, you'll find many good ideas to make your closets more accommodating and to make you feel better about your wardrobe—and yourself.

The closet that comes with the home you move into—unless specifically designed otherwise—is likely to be either a roomy walk-in closet (especially in an older home) or a shallow, but lengthy, wall closet. Both have particular advantages. In general, clotheshorses prefer the walk-in style, simply because

it usually holds more (see pages 36 and 37). Of course, with good space planning and double-decker closet rods, a wall closet can accommodate the most extensive collection of clothing. Some fine examples appear on pages 34 and 35.

And then there's the matter of doors. Here walkins have another advantage: a standard door that can usually carry accessories on specialized racks and hooks. Wall closets are most often equipped with sliding doors. These can be vexing, either because they occasionally jam or slip off their tracks or just because they never disclose a full view of a wardrobe. Accordion-fold doors, made of two or more hinged panels, are preferable. These fold back to each side, so you can review your closet's contents with one sweeping glance. But any closet door—standard, sliding, or accordion-fold—will be more effective if it's also louvered for ventilation.

Have you ever considered using a closet *without* doors? We show this new approach to clothing storage—the unabashed open look—on pages 38 and 39.

If you have space for a dressing area (or a separate dressing room), you'll find plenty of ideas for organizing and decorating it on pages 42 through 45. Some dressing areas can even perform a dual role. The one on page 44, for example, doubles as a laundry/ sewing room; the dressing room shown on page 45 also serves as an exercise studio.

Maybe you spend vacations at a small mountain cabin, or have college-age children who drop in, temporarily, at home. In either case, you'll find some useful ideas on pages 52 and 53, which are devoted to temporary and portable closets.

Is your youngster's closet a jumble of toys and crumpled clothing? Some delightful ideas for organizing kids' clothes quarters can be found on pages 40 and 41.

Carefully planning your closet storage means avoiding wasted space. Throughout this section you'll notice that closet rods are doubled; most of our apparel nowadays simply doesn't need the full 64-inch height generally provided by the single pole that is standard in traditional closets.

Having saved space with double-decker rods, you may be able to fit in several levels of shelves, drawers, or pull-out bins (see pages 32 and 33). In this chapter, you'll see how bins of vinyl-coated wire have the triple advantages of cheerful good looks, maximum ventilation, and quick visibility of contents.

Shoes need shelving, too, so allow them an appropriate amount of closet space. Stored up off the floor, your footwear stays bright and dust-free. And you'll find it's much less frustrating to slide a vacuum cleaner quickly across an uncluttered closet floor.

Accessories also need places to call their own. Look at pages 48 and 49 for clever ideas on organizing them with special hangers, custom racks, baskets and barrels, and hooks and pegs.

To combat that closet pest, the moth, who has been dining on silks and woolens since they were first woven, you can line the closet with cedar, an effective but expensive solution. Or you can use repellent, taking care to keep it out of the reach of children.

After you've organized your closet and before you fill it once again, review your wardrobe, sorting it by categories of "Absolutely love this," "Not sure," and "Why did I buy this?" By keeping only the first two categories, you'll look—and feel—much better in your clothing.

A Closet System

Open shelves, drawers, and multilevel rods
work together to organize your clothes quarters

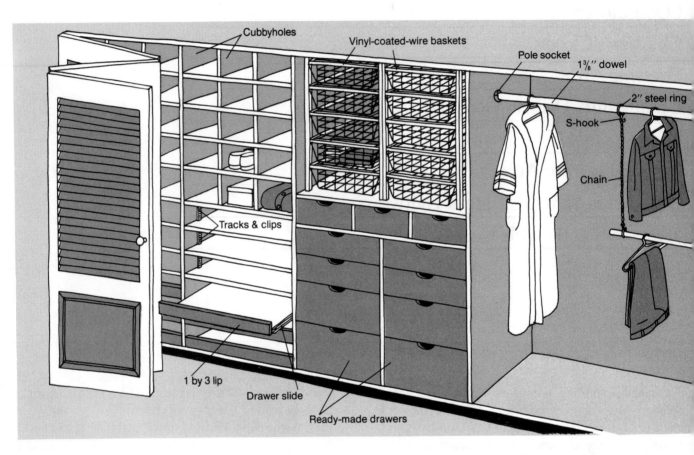

Open shelves

Shelves are probably the most versatile components in a closet system. They accommodate items in a wide variety of shapes and sizes (from ten-gallon hats to handkerchiefs); they keep stored items visible; and they're easy to install. And if you use an adjustable system of tracks and clips or tracks and brackets, shelves are also easy to rearrange.

Fir and pine are good choices for closet shelving; so are ¾-inch plywood and particle board, especially if your shelves will be deeper than 12 inches. If you're planning a shelf longer than 4 feet (3 feet if it's particle board), be sure to add a mid-span support.

For added interest—and convenience—use vertical dividers to form clusters of cubbyholes, or convert some of your shelves to pull-outs by adding standard drawer slides and lipped edges made from 1 by 3s.

Drawers & pull-outs

Simplify your dressing routine—and gain valuable floor space in the bedroom—by eliminating your bulky bureau and adding a new drawer system in the closet. If you want a built-in unit, construct a frame to accommodate ready-made drawers (available in many sizes). Or buy a modular set of drawers. For visible storage, try a system of vinyl-coated-wire bins that glide in and out on their own framework.

Multilevel rods

In updated closets, the primary space waster—the traditional single closet rod—has given way to multiple rods whose heights are determined by the owner's clothing. But you needn't make any major structural changes to convert your closet to multilevel rods. Just buy an adjustable suspension bar, or make one of your own from a metal bar or wood dowel, steel rings, S-hooks, and some lightweight chain (as shown).

Closet metamorphosis

Before the new storage system was installed (see inset), this all-too-typical closet broke virtually every rule for good closet design and organization. Its one long shelf was crammed with hats and handbags, books and bedding, while the extra foot of space between the shelf items and the ceiling above was totally unused. Clothes were jammed together on the one long closet rod, which was low enough to make long dresses and robes dust the floor, yet high enough to leave several feet of wasted space below jackets, skirts, and blouses. Impossible to vacuum, the closet floor was a dusty jumble of shoes, boots, handbags, and luggage.

With the new organizers in place, the closet holds everything it did before—and more—with room to spare. Five different levels of closet rods make sure that each item gets the space it needs. The closet floor is clear (and dust-free) now that shoes and handbags are lined up on shelves of their own. And, best of all, the owners were able to eliminate their bulky bedroom bureau—thanks to a stack of large-capacity closet drawers and some roomy open shelves for sweaters and other foldables. Closet interior: Just Closets.

Wall Closets

A custom design can double—even triple—
your closet's storage potential

Wardrobe at a glance

Many of us have closets we're only too glad to shut the door on. But this one offers a compartmentalized network so neat that it's actually pleasing to contemplate from the vantage point of one's bed at 6 A.M. (The slide-out tie rack just to the right of the mirrored center panel is shown more closely on page 48.)

When the bifold doors are closed, an expanse of mirrors not only aids grooming but creates the illusion of doubled room depth. Design: Alan Lucas & Associates.

Planning ingenuity creates a closet for two

A little engineering carved ample storage for both his wardrobe and hers in a relatively compact space—leaving the rest of this bedroom serenely uncluttered. Baskets of vinyl-coated wire offer several advantages over traditional, and bulky, chests of drawers: they allow ventilation, they make it easier to find your favorite pullover, and—most of the time—they hide neatly behind the closet doors. Architect: N. Kent Linn. Interior design: Joan Simon.

Predawn efficiency

For many a commuter, every morning minute counts in the race to catch the train, bus, or carpool, and an efficiently arranged closet like this one can pare down dressing time and ease those important first decisions of the day. Thanks to the bifold doors, even sleep-filled eyes can take in most of the wardrobe at a glance. In the center of the closet, accessible from both sets of doors, are two rods offering double-decker storage for shirts, jackets, and slacks; at the far left, longer coats and robes hang at standard height. Shoe shelves eliminate floor clutter, and a stack of drawers and open shelves keeps folded shirts and other clothing in good order. Closet interior: Just Closets.

Cozy cache in a corner

Like the intricate honeycomb of a hard-working beehive, this remodeled high-and-narrow Victorian closet leaves scarcely a centimeter to chance disorder. New double-decker closet rods carry twice the freight of the original single one, and the newly installed bank of open shelves accommodates volumes of sweaters and other foldables without crush or confusion. Closet interior: Just Closets.

Walk-in Closets

Luxurious spots to shelter a wardrobe—some so spacious they double as dressing rooms

Within easy reach of the bath

Housing your garments adjacent to the bathroom can save flurry and flutter as you race the clock on weekday mornings.

Such convenience was feasible here without threat of moisture damage to the wardrobe. The spacious bathroom is well ventilated (a must for this kind of arrangement), and a sliding door seals off the adjoining closet.

Lighting for the closet is supplied by fluorescent tubes above the cornices. Architects: Designbank.

High-rise housing for clothing foldables

Good-looking enough to display books or collectibles, the wall unit at one end of this spacious walk-in is a private cache for quantities of foldable clothing. Cubbyholes at mid-level hold clear acrylic bins full of small items such as socks and lingerie. Double rods along one side of the closet, double shelves and a rod along the other, accommodate two extensive wardrobes neatly and without crowding. Design: Philip Emminger.

For clotheshorses, a spacious livery stable

Most walk-in closets are big enough to comfortably accommodate wardrobes for two people—even when each person makes frequent sartorial acquisitions. In this closet, there's space for floor-to-ceiling shoe shelves, a built-in chest of drawers, and a necktie rack. Double closet rods on either side offer an uncrowded abundance of raiment. And everything is easy to see—thanks to good indirect fluorescent lighting. Architect: Ron Yeo.

Open Closets

Honest, upfront clothes quarters to flaunt your finery

Letting it all hang out

Tucked under an eave, a man's collection of striped, plaid, and tattersall clothing makes an unobtrusive, tidy display that pleases the eye and detracts not a whit from the bedroom's striking design. During the day, skylights illuminate clothing colors; when the sun goes down, that function is performed by wall-mounted fixtures that look like jumbo dressing-table lights.

Above the closet is a compartment with sliding doors; to the left is a tall built-in unit with a white-enameled cabinet topping a dozen black-lacquered drawers. Architect: Wendell Lovett. Interior design: Suzanne Braddock.

Haberdashery, unabashedly on display

Looking something like an opened-up steamer trunk, this movable wall unit holds a man's wardrobe in natty good order. A covering curtain or screen for the closet would only make this small bedroom seem smaller. But as an honest display—sporting neckties like pennants and crowned with crisscrossed tennis rackets—this arrangement serves as a personal haberdashery, letting the owner make mental selections before he even gets out of bed. Closet design: Just Closets.

Two wardrobes separate bed and bath

Curved and compact, this room divider doubles as an open armoire for two people. Reminiscent of the voluptuous furniture styles of the 1930s, the closet curiosity has room for everything from brogues to silk dresses. The curved section offers open shelving, necktie pegs, a pull-out bin for laundry, and deep drawers of clear acrylic for small foldable items. Around the bend, facing the bathroom, there are additional nooks and crannies for towels and toiletries. Architect: Gary Allen.

Children's Closets

Organizing kids' clothes quarters for easy upkeep

Closet revamp encourages tidiness

With all his personal effects piled in a jumble, either on
the floor or high up out of reach, it was hard for the
eight-year-old owner of this closet to find things or put
them away (see inset, right). But built-in shelves and
drawers, plus an extra closet rod placed at just the right
height for him, brought order out of frustrating chaos. At
the same time, as with any well-planned closet remodel,
space was cleared for storing at least twice as much. Closet
interior: Just Closets.

Small girl's wardrobe makes a fetching display

Her mother's serendipitous shopping trips turned up unusual and elegant organizers for a five-year-old's wardrobe. Pretty hats and colorful dresses hang from an antique coat rack. Below that, a handsome wooden towel rack from a bath accessory boutique holds everyday play clothes. And, most imaginatively, her small-scale footwear lodges in a divided wicker desk tray originally designed to hold stationery. The entire arrangement makes a charming display in a small bedroom that has no built-in closet.

Nooks for Baby's needs

Naked we come into this world—but we don't stay that way for long. Before you can say "Dr. Spock," most babies have acquired a veritable mountain of clothes, linens, and other possessions. To stow it all in orderly fashion may be one of the first major challenges of parenthood.

In this nursery closet, there's a nook for every need. A short, low closet rod encourages Baby, as she grows, to hang up her own clothes. Baskets of vinyl-coated wire allow both ventilation and easy viewing of contents. Architect: N. Kent Linn. Interior design: Joan Simon.

Dressing Areas

Create a corner—or a luxurious separate room—
where you can retire to attire

Plenty of doors and drawers

Behind the large double doors in this dressing room,
you'll find a tidy double-rod clothes closet; behind the
smaller doors are individual cubbyholes for as many as
thirty pairs of shoes. Below the counter, built-in drawers
of varying depths provide streamlined accommodation for
folded items. Architect: Charles L. Howell.

Athletic esthetics

Dubbed "The Locker Room," this spacious dressing hall
features an amenity not often included in dressing-area design. Down its considerable length runs a sturdy locker-room
bench, crafted of wood. Beyond its good looks, it provides
a place to sit for lacing up running shoes or toweling off after
a shower.

Other noteworthy features are a full-length mirror (with
plenty of room to back away for a long look), adjustable
track lights, a Chinese basket that functions as a clothes
hamper, and—of course—an efficiently arranged closet with
double-decker rods and adjustable open shelves. Architects:
Rachlin Architects.

Reflections on the art of dressing

Look beyond the stunning hammered brass sink and brass-trimmed tile counter, and you're aware of something equally impressive reflected in the mirror: a spacious closet on the opposite wall of the dressing room proudly displays its beautifully stacked, stored, and suspended wares. Louvered for both good looks and good ventilation, its trifold doors hinge back to reveal an entire wardrobe. Architect: David Jeremiah Hurley. Interior design: Jois.

Horseshoe headboard creates a dressing corridor

Unless you're back there deciding on something to wear, you don't notice the expansive wardrobe accommodations formed by this tall, horseshoe-shaped headboard. Placed toward one end of the bedroom, the arrangement creates a private dressing corridor—narrow, but with comfortable elbow room for pulling on a turtleneck, zipping into a dress, or lacing up shoes. Other behind-the-headboard dressing areas are shown on pages 12 and 13. Architects: Jacobson and Silverstein.

Double-duty Dressing Rooms

Stretching beyond their usefulness as places to don your duds

Bedroom annex is a clothing-care center

Dressing with both care and efficiency is easier when you keep your clothes and all the appliances needed for their upkeep in one handy location. This combination dressing-laundry-sewing room includes open shelves, drawers, closets (not shown), a washer and dryer, sewing machine, and fold-away ironing board. All are ready for instant service, whether you need to store, wash, dry, or repair your clothing—or just press something at the last minute. Architects: Olsen/Walker. Cabinetry: The Butt Joint.

Next to the bath, a home figure salon

Everything a body might need to keep in shape is right here—doctor's scale; expansive mirrors for checking apparel—or one's ballet posture; an exercise bar for morning workouts (it's mounted with strong handrail brackets); and a tall chest full of clothing to put on a newly trimmed-down, toned-up figure. On the right (behind the scale) is a closet for hanging garments. Architect: Jennifer Clements.

Dressing Tables

Sitting down to all the accouterments of good grooming

Chic import swings open for your toilette

Displaying its wares from cleverly swiveling trays, this portable make-up center conceals all the trappings of good grooming within a trim plastic façade. And there's even more storage potential inside the padded vinyl stool. A costly import from Italy, this handsome vanity pivots and folds together when not in use, its compartmentalized trays, mirror, and storage seat transformed into a sleek stack.

Cosmetics corner

Find an empty corner and fill it—this is one of the fundamentals of clever storage. Here, a custom-designed dressing table turns an otherwise wasted bedroom corner into an essential part of its owner's grooming regimen. Decoratively paneled bins swivel out from the wall to proffer their cargo of cosmetics, then swivel back under the vanity shelf. The triple mirror is framed with the same oak detailing that decorates the drawers.

The romantic allure of wicker

An appealing beginning— and end—to each day are practically guaranteed at this charming little wicker vanity. Its simple, arched design catches the eye and may even divert attention from the clutter that all dressing tables inevitably collect. The unobtrusive glass shelves are easy to wipe clean. Furniture courtesy of de Benedictis Showrooms.

For today's fair lady, antique beauty

"The Fair each moment rises in her Charms/Repairs her Smiles, awakens ev'ry Grace/And calls forth all the Wonders of her Face." So wrote Alexander Pope early in the 18th century, addressing himself to the mysteries of a lady's toilette. For many of us, such marvelous transformations would be aided by an inspirational setting. Here's the very thing—an elegant Louis Philippe vanity with upholstered bench, both crafted of walnut. Lighting— essential to any dressing table—is stylishly supplied by smartly draped windows and a pair of lamps.

47

Organizing Your Accessories

Use baskets and barrels, hangers and holders
to arrange those all-important extras

Fold-up, slide-away tie ladder

The sides of this ladder rack swing up for easy access
to more than four dozen ties on six dowels. Once the tie
selection is made, the sides swing back down for compact storage. The entire unit slips in and out of the
closet on standard drawer slides. Design: Alan Lucas &
Associates.

Hidden jewelry storage

Tucked away in the back of a closet and concealed behind hanging garments is this clever hideaway for
jewelry. Built between the wall studs, the cabinet houses
eight fabric-lined, shallow drawers. For camouflage, the
outside of the cabinet door is painted the same color
as the rest of the closet wall, and the door opens by
means of a touch-latch. Design: Philip Emminger.

Put baskets & barrels to work as handy holders

Use baskets—wire or woven—to organize socks, lingerie, gloves, and scarves. Place them on closet shelves, tuck them into drawers, or suspend them from the closet ceiling.

Try a fiber drum, a small wine barrel, or an enameled metal drum to hold those tall, skinny items that are propped up precariously in the back corners of your closet: umbrellas, walking sticks, and sports equipment such as fishing rods, skis, baseball bats, and hockey sticks.

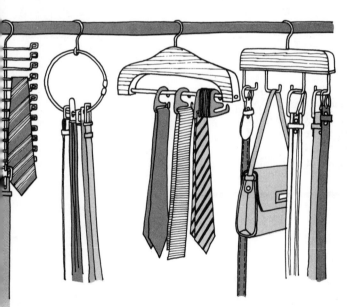

Hangers that major in accessories

Some smart-looking accessory holders, like the ones shown here, are designed to slip right over the closet rod. Available in the notions sections of most department stores or through mail-order catalogs, these specialty hangers hold belts, ties, scarves, handbags, or various combinations of accessories.

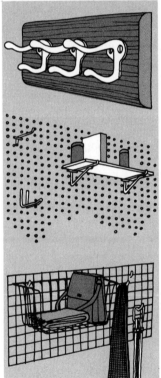

Closet hang-ups

Stylish or mundane, a system of hang-ups in your closet can organize and display belts, ties, scarves, hats, handbags, and even necklaces. You might use simple plastic holders with adhesive backing, an antique oak taproom rack with fancy brass hooks, or a high-tech grid system of vinyl-coated wire.

Improvised hooks and pegs are equally effective; try china knobs, cabinet pulls, old railroad spikes, or even common carpenter's nails.

Organizing Your Clothing & Footwear

Keep your wardrobe under control with these inexpensive closet products and easy-to-build storage aids

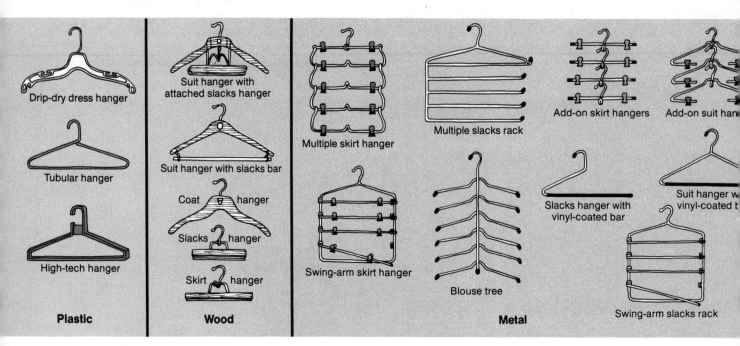

Drip-dry dress hanger

Tubular hanger

High-tech hanger

Plastic

Suit hanger with attached slacks hanger

Suit hanger with slacks bar

Coat hanger

Slacks hanger

Skirt hanger

Wood

Multiple skirt hanger

Swing-arm skirt hanger

Multiple slacks rack

Blouse tree

Metal

Add-on skirt hangers

Add-on suit han

Slacks hanger with vinyl-coated bar

Suit hanger w vinyl-coated b

Swing-arm slacks rack

Trade in those wire hangers

Do your clothes a favor and discard the wire hangers you've collected over the years from dry cleaners and laundries. Never meant for long-term use, they crease folded slacks, misshape garment shoulders, and sag under the weight of winter coats and heavy jackets. Worst of all, they seem to multiply in your closet and always end up in a tangle. Why not replace them with colorful plastic hangers—or wood or metal hangers designed for particular garments?

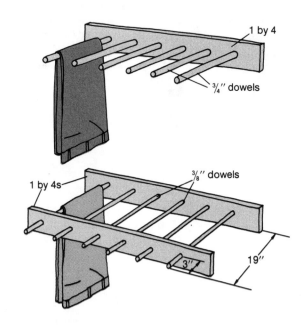

1 by 4

¾″ dowels

1 by 4s

⅜″ dowels

3″

19″

Easy-to-build slacks rack

Your closet gains a custom touch with the addition of a simple slacks rack. To build the horizontal ladder shown, run 19-inch lengths of ⅜-inch doweling through corresponding holes in parallel 1 by 4s; allow the dowels to protrude 3 inches beyond the front 1 by 4 to form accessory pegs. Secure the dowels with white glue spread inside each drilled hole. Choose a ladder length that fits between opposing closet walls or vertical dividers. The rear 1 by 4 is fastened to wall studs with 3-inch-long lag screws; then the front is attached to both walls with angle brackets.

If you'd rather slide your slacks onto a rack from the front (instead of looping them over from above), attach ¾-inch dowels to a back 1 by 4 only.

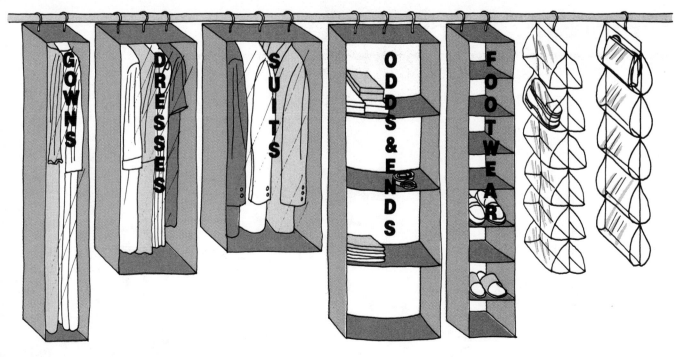

Hanging garment bags are practical protectors

For storage of shoes, hats, handbags, and out-of-season or seldom used clothing, consider purchasing a handy hanging garment bag—or a whole matching set of them. Bags made for clothing on hangers are sized for long evening wear, dresses, or suits; accessory bags with shelves come in two sizes—one for shoes, and one for hats, handbags, sweaters, and other bulky items. Made from clear, colored, or patterned vinyl, the bags have front or side zippers for easy access.

Also available on hangers are vinyl organizers with pockets for shoes or handbags.

You'll find garment and accessory bags in the notions sections of large department stores or in mail-order catalogs.

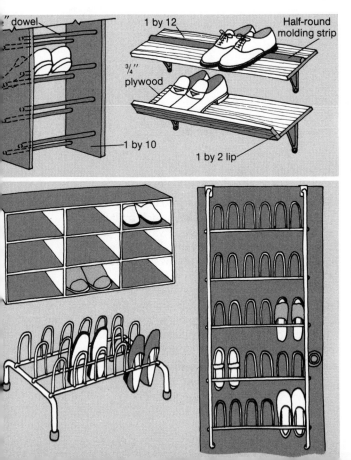

Footnote on shoe storage

Among the chief contributors to closet clutter are shoes. If you store them on the closet floor, sometimes it's a chore just to dig out two that match, and when you do, they may be covered with dust. Ready-made shoe racks (over-the-door models, floor racks, vinyl wall pouches) can solve these "pedi" problems. Or, with some inexpensive materials, a few simple tools, and a little know-how, you can put together a custom rack of your own.

Shoe shelves are easy to build from 1 by 12 lumber or ¾-inch plywood. Use regular L-brackets to hang them right on the wall, or use straight or angled brackets in an adjustable track-and-bracket system; with the latter you can make slanting shelves. Add a half-round molding strip as a heel stop (see illustration), or, if your shelves are made of plywood, put a 1 by 2 lip along the front to keep shoes from sliding and to hide the plywood edge. (Since there's no overhang, be sure your lipped shelves are at least as deep as your shoes are long.)

Another good choice is a dowel rack—reaching to the ceiling, if you like. First, cut two side pieces from a pine or fir 1 by 10, then drill holes for pairs of ½-inch dowels, offsetting them (as shown) for a forward tilt.

Temporary & Portable Closets

Versatile storage pieces on hand when you need them—
and out of the way when you don't

Movable closets serve as a room divider

These practical units allow you to convert a spacious room, such as a family room or
large bedroom, into two private sleeping areas—without making any structural
changes. What's more, they provide each sleeping area with a roomy closet of its own.

Built from $\frac{3}{4}$-inch plywood, each of the units shown here is 40 inches wide, 24 inches
deep, and $3\frac{3}{4}$ inches shorter than ceiling height. (Of course, you can adjust these dimensions—or add additional units—as necessary.) Each closet has a tall space with a
rod for hanging clothing, and a two-shelf cabinet above for shoes, hats, and bulky
sweaters.

The closets are brought into the room on a dolly and slid into position on a continu-
ous sill built from 2 by 4s, with one unit facing into each sleeping area. Since the 2 by 4
sill is actually $3\frac{1}{2}$ inches high, you'll have just enough overhead clearance ($\frac{1}{4}$ inch)
for a tight fit. For extra stability, the units can be secured to the ceiling with molding
strips or angle brackets.

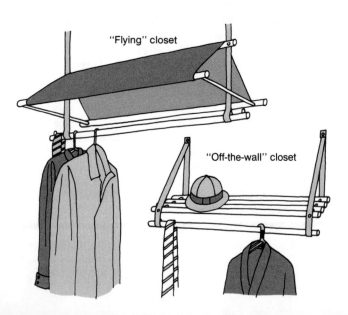

"Flying" closet

"Off-the-wall" closet

Suspended storage

Here are two commercially available hanging closets
that are easy to carry and quick to install.

The "off-the-wall" closet has a shelf built from
natural-finish hardwood dowels with another dowel
suspended below as a closet rod. The whole assembly
hangs from natural-color cotton webbing straps that are
attached to the wall studs.

The "flying" closet is suspended on cotton webbing
from two mounting hooks screwed into the ceiling joists.
Garments hanging on the wooden closet rod are protected
from dust by an attractive natural-color canvas awning.
Closet designs: Richard Pathman.

Almost-instant closets

Empty corners in a bedroom are prime quick-closet candidates. Simply install a shelf on the diagonal, suspend a closet rod from it, and close off the triangular area with blinds, curtains, or a Roman shade. If you prefer traditional doors, build a frame from 2 by 4s covered with plywood strips or wallboard.

Other quick-closet ideas: hide a commercial garment rack behind a beautiful folding screen, or try the original open closet—the coat tree.

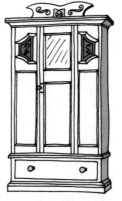

Antique wooden wardrobe

Contemporary wardrobe of plastic laminate

Freestanding wardrobes go where they're needed

Whether they're carved and mirrored antiques, sleek contemporary pieces of glossy plastic laminate, or inexpensive metal-framed cardboard units, freestanding wardrobes are as practical as ever. The original portable closets, they're a solution for bedrooms with little or no built-in closet space.

Metal-framed cardboard wardrobe

Bathroom Storage

O f all the rooms in the house, the bathroom tends to be the smallest—and the least seriously considered in terms of effective space planning. Yet, in recent decades, many of us have begun to collect more and more paraphernalia (including bulky electrical grooming appliances) that we use most often in the bathroom.

Your answers to the following questions will help you plan your bathroom storage requirements: What supplies do you need and use regularly in the bathroom besides a toothbrush, soap, and towels? Many people store cosmetics, medicines, small appliances, extra toilet and facial tissue, magazines and books, and cleaning supplies. Can the items you use regularly be housed conveniently in your present bathroom storage space? If not, you'll welcome this chapter's wealth of practical and attractive solutions to bath storage problems.

When it comes to basic bathroom storage units— cabinets and drawers—you have a wide range of materials, styles, and colors to choose from. Some new designs in traditional wood cabinetry are shown on pages 58 and 59, and on pages 60 and 61 you'll find some of the sleek European imports of plastic laminate. If you're thinking of building your own cabinetry, you can get ideas and instructions from these *Sunset* books: *Basic Carpentry Illustrated*, *Bookshelves & Cabinets*, and *Wall Systems & Shelving*.

Is the inside of your cabinetry as hardworking as it could be? On pages 56 and 57 we show ideas for storing supplies in racks, pull-outs, and lazy Susans that hide behind cabinet doors.

You'd rather *display* colorful towels and stacks of soap than tuck them behind closed doors? Take a look at the attractive open shelving on pages 62 and 63.

Medicine cabinets are a standard feature in bathrooms, but your medicine cabinet needn't be humdrum if you choose one of the novel designs or arrangements presented on pages 66 and 67. Laundry hamper ideas appear on pages 70 and 71. And for housing the burgeoning number of appliances that shave, curl, tweeze, or dry your hair, improve complexions, and clean teeth, see the ideas on pages 76 and 77.

On pages 74 and 75 you'll see a selection of towel racks to buy or make. And on pages 72 and 73 we offer an equally fine selection of racks for paperbacks and periodicals.

Provided the room has adequate space and ventilation, you may choose to store your linens in or near the bathroom. You'll find some examples of effective and modern linen closets on pages 64 and 65.

Take a good look around your bathroom. Search for potential storage space in now-wasted areas. Likely locations include the space between the medicine chest and the sink, the space above the toilet (leave 12 inches above the tank for servicing the mechanism), corners that you could fill with triangular units, and the bathroom door on which you can install hooks, pegs, racks, or baskets.

What about that empty space above the tub? Either narrow cabinets or open shelves placed above the bathtub will dramatically expand your bathroom storage capacity. One caveat: Make sure the storage units and the items to be stored are impervious to moisture. Nothing dampens the spirits more than clinging bath powder or flaking paint from improperly finished cabinetry.

If moisture isn't a problem in your bathroom, and if you have space to spare, you might consider moving in furniture—an attractive old chest or bookcase can add good looks as well as storage.

As in planning your bedroom or reorganizing your closets, what will work best for you really depends on what you need and use frequently, how much space you have to work with, and what resources are available. Whether you build or buy your storage units or hire a design consultant, your best resource is your own imagination, combined with practical ingenuity.

Cabinetry: The "Inside" Story

Clutter-swallowing helpers that hide behind closed cabinet doors

Problem-solving pull-outs

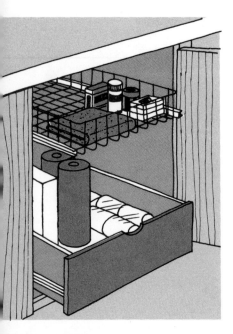

There's no need to grope around in your bathroom cabinets in search of that extra tube of toothpaste or the bubble bath you got last Christmas. With pull-outs like the ones shown here, bath supplies glide right out for easy access. Available in wood, regular and vinyl-coated wire, and plastic, pull-outs can be installed on standard drawer slides or on their own special framework.

Back-of-the-door bonanza

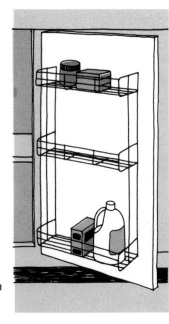

A wood or vinyl-coated-wire storage rack mounted to the inside of a cabinet door can help you organize soaps, shampoos, and other cosmetics, as well as bathroom cleaning supplies.

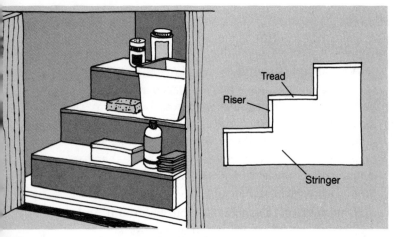

Bath-supply bleachers

This generous grandstand for bath supplies assures that nothing will be overlooked in the back of the cabinet. Graduated storage steps put an emphasis on visibility: you see your entire inventory of paper products and cosmetics at a glance.

Once you've designed a bleacher unit to fit your needs—and your cabinet—cut treads and risers from 1-inch lumber and stringers from ½-inch plywood. With finishing nails, assemble the pieces as shown; coat the unit with varnish or enamel, then slide it into place inside your cabinet.

Not-so-lazy Susans

These hard-working storage-go-rounds help keep bathroom paraphernalia from finding its way into the far reaches of your cabinetry. Single-level or tiered, a lazy Susan rotates so that everything you store is visible and accessible. Be sure to measure your cabinet carefully—allowing for drainpipe clearance, if necessary—before you buy or build one of these organizers.

These cabinets put away plenty

Imported from Germany, this plastic laminate bath cabinetry carries all the soaps, cleansers, lotions, creams, and scents you'll need for some time to come. The gleaming chrome towel rack swings out of the way to allow easy access to the spacious undersink compartment; the cabinet on the left features swivel-out trays in various sizes. Cabinetry courtesy of European Kitchens & Baths.

A parade of pull-outs

Hidden most of the time behind closed doors, these under-the-sink pull-outs glide into clear view when you need to get at their contents. Ranging from deep bins to shallow sliding shelves, they serve up everything from daintily folded guest towels to scented dusting powder. Topping the wooden cabinetry is a counter of blue plastic laminate; the glamorous basin is made of brushed aluminum.

Cabinetry of Wood

The traditional raw material of the cabinetmaker's art, shown here in designs that are far from ordinary.

A touch of the peaceful East

Oriental influence is serenely apparent in the soft-toned simplicity of the wood detailing, the spacious proportions, and the quietly beautiful tile design that draw the mind away from the cares of a busy day. In addition to the traditional undersink cabinet and bank of drawers, there is a generous tiled dressing bench with a single substantial drawer below for linens. Cabinet design: The Butt Joint

Hollywood glamour, right at home

Curving cabinetry and theatrical make-up lights add star quality to this sleek sink and storage area. The mirrored panels at either end of the unit are actually mirror-faced doors for twin medicine cabinets. And below the sink, a cupboard and bank of drawers offer roomy recesses for tucking away towels, lotions, and other accouterments of glamorous grooming. Architects: Olsen/Walker. Cabinet design: The Butt Joint.

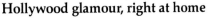

Orderly without, organized within

There's nothing trendy about this bathroom storage wall and sink counter. The attractive traditional-style wood cabinetry and a mirrored medicine cabinet just look great and do their job—keeping bath necessities and even clothing in their proper place—while giving the whole room a pleasing sense of order. Who could ask for more? When open to view, the drawers and doors disclose a wealth of storage organization, including a roomy set of wooden pull-outs. Design: Dennis O'Connor.

Cabinetry of Plastic Laminate

The sleek, chic European imports
are a bold new bath-storage option

**Plastic pizzazz,
Italian-style**

From the ultra-modern
approach of northern Italian
design comes this factory-
molded sculptural elegance
for the bathroom. The clever
countertop towel rack whim-
sically plays with terrycloth
tones, creating vertical stripes
that balance the horizontal
strokes of navy blue on the
wall above. Drawers and
cabinets are anything but
boring—they're concave or
convex; they can be pulled
or swiveled. And even the
vanity stool stands for more
than just plain seating—it
stores things, too. Cabinetry
courtesy of Dahl Designs.

Wall-covering cabinetry

This German cabinetry puts every square inch of a bathroom wall to work—with precision. The fine-lined pattern on drawers and cabinet doors provides an interesting texture that's resistant to fingerprints, as well. Behind the beautiful façade are cleverly designed interiors to accommodate everything from cosmetics to laundry. (You can peek behind the doors on pages 57 and 71.) Cabinetry courtesy of European Kitchens & Baths.

Not corners, but curves

This sand and charcoal-colored cabinetry presents a rounded look that's a refreshing contrast to the harsher, predominantly angular environment of many bathrooms. So there are no handles to interrupt the smooth façade, all cabinets open with touch-latches. The bottom cabinet on the far side (shown open) features a swing-out towel rack. Cabinetry courtesy of Dahl Designs.

Open Shelves

Out-in-the-open storage puts towels
and other bright bath supplies on display

Tubside art enhances the bath

Surely one of the most sumptuous of life's simple pleasures is a good, hot soak in a bubbly bath. To enrich the experience, this bathroom provides a colorful gallery of miniature folk art for bathtime viewing. Besides display space, the handsome cedar shelves offer storage for bright towels, and even for a few books. Architect: William Abbott.

Towels sit high up in brassy splendor

In days gone by, this vintage piece held luggage overhead in a cramped train compartment. Today, in a crowded bathroom, it keeps extra towels out of the way, yet within reach. Its brass mesh shelf and filigree framing are a treat to view from underneath. Design: Rand Hughes.

Greenhouse windows offer shelf space

Greenhouse popouts, available from building-supply and home-improvement centers, can provide extra space and daylight, as well as wide views of the leafy world outside. At the same time, they offer attractive shelf space for both practical and decorative items. Since the room faces a shady corner of the garden, there's no worry that sunlight might fade the towels. Design: Woody Dike.

Mini-library for private browsing

Many people appreciate the privacy bathrooms afford for reading in undistracted solitude. Here, a colorful collection of paperbacks offers not only food for thought, but hospitality and decorative cheer as well. You'll find more ideas for bathroom libraries on pages 72–73. Design: Jeanne Kleyn.

Graceful niche for bath necessities

An arched alcove, traversed by a single glass shelf, creates open wall storage with a clean and airy feeling. The rectangular opening just below houses a fluorescent light behind a frosted glass panel; more glass functions as sliding doors for the base cabinet.

Under the window, a laundry hamper disguises itself as a simple ledge when its lid is closed. Architects: Ted Tanaka and Frank Purtill.

Linen Closets

Orderly accommodation for the bulk of your bed and bath needs

Closet chic

Clean-as-a-whistle white shelving etches a crisp border around stacked sheets and towels in this walk-in linen closet.

Derived from an industrial design, these vinyl-coated-wire shelves are available for the home through specialty shops, interior designers, and home centers. Besides their look of high-tech sophistication, they offer other advantages: good air circulation, light weight, quick installation, and easy access to their contents. Architect: John Galbraith.

Sleek exterior, hard-working interior

One basic aim of good storage design is an everything-in-place look that's gentle on the eyes. When all its doors and drawers are closed, this floor-to-ceiling storage wall blends unobtrusively into its all-white bathroom surroundings—only the glistening brass hardware calls attention to its function. Behind the cabinet doors, colorful linens are neatly arranged on lipped, pull-out shelves. Architects: Fisher/Friedman Associates. Interior design: Randee Seiger.

Stowaway space, unlimited

This meticulously planned storage wall swallows more than enough linens to meet the bed and bath requirements of even a large family.

Cabinets midway up the wall feature doors that swing down on piano hinges to become counters just right for folding and sorting laundry. Adjustable shelves inside the upper cabinets provide flexible storage spaces. Architect: John Galbraith.

Medicine Cabinets

Handy, high-style housing for home remedies
and prescriptions, first-aid supplies and cosmetics

Pops open at a touch

Just give this medicine
cabinet door a little push
and it'll pop right open—
thanks to the convenient
touch-latch. Since the door
opens upward, you'll
want to position the cabinet low enough for adults'
convenience, but high
enough to prevent
bumped foreheads. Cabi-
net courtesy of Plus
Kitchens.

Low-lying cabinets leave room for a view

For many of us, the first sight of the day, as we splash cold water on our faces, is somewhat
less inspiring than a gentle garden view. But as this thoughtful arrangement makes
clear, the traditional over-the-sink mirror is not compulsory. Here, you can have it both
ways: twin medicine cabinets with mirrored sliding doors are recessed into the back-
splash area, leaving space for a window above one sink and for a mirror above the other.
Architects: Ted Tanaka and Frank Purtill.

Prescription for storage

Built in between the wall studs, this wooden medicine chest is compact yet roomy, with storage space on the inside of the cabinet door as well as on the interior shelves. Small-diameter wooden dowels keep door-stored items in place. Design: Jeanne Kleyn.

Cabinet puts corner to work

Tucked into a corner between the sink and bathtub, this jumbo medicine cabinet holds cosmetics, remedies, and bath supplies for the whole family. Below it is a tip-out laundry hamper (you see it open on page 70). Architect: William B. Remick.

Showerside Storage

A berth for every bathing need

Tile frames supplies—and scenery

Bright blue tiles wrap the storage niches and window that make this tub/shower combination special—as well as convenient for family use. Plastic tub toys, soap, and hair care needs are right at hand, and the glimpse of the outdoors is a bonus. Architects: Fisher/Friedman Associates. Interior design: Randee Seiger.

Towels greet you as you round the bend

Just around the corner is a roomy shower, tiled in bright white from floor to ceiling. But here, tucked in a tall, tiled recess, are thick and thirsty towels that stay well out of moisture's way—yet handy for drying you off as you emerge dripping from a steaming shower. Design: Philip Emminger.

Shower heads have hang-ups, too

Short of perching your shower supplies precariously on a windowsill or tub ledge, no storage system could be simpler than this clear acrylic device that slips over and hangs from the shower head. Available in department stores and bath boutiques, shower caddies usually have a small rack for a washcloth, a ribbed tray for soap, and a shelf that's slanted to keep water from pooling under the shampoo bottles.

Sheer beauty from Italy

Imported from Italy and sold for a pretty American penny, this prefabricated cylindrical shower stall comes with storage compartments as sleek-looking as those racy Italian sports cars. While you're getting wet, the towels and toiletries stay dry behind a curved, clear acrylic sliding panel. Architect: William B. Remick.

Hampers & Scales

A fresh, new look at those bathroom basics

Hatch lifts up to catch clothing

The sturdy fir deck around this bathtub provides more than just good-looking surroundings for a sudsy soak. It also makes efficient use of the space between the tub and a wall by offering a roomy built-in laundry hamper. When the lid is closed, the spot doubles as a dressing bench. Design: James Fey.

Tip-out bin for a tight spot

In this bathroom, a tip-out laundry bin takes clever advantage of the corner between the sink and bathtub. It serves its purpose smoothly in a tight-cornered room where a conventional freestanding hamper would only be in the way. Architect: William B. Remick.

For towel-tossing

Flip open this sleek tilt-down cabinet door and you find a laundry hamper just waiting for you to play doff-and-toss. The vinyl-coated-wire basket lifts out so that after you've flung your clothing and towels into it, you can carry the whole works over to the washer. Cabinetry courtesy of European Kitchens & Baths.

Between truth sessions, scale disappears

Mommy and Daddy might cringe to read what they weigh, but to a youngster it's a real thrill to gain a pound or two. This young lady stands on a niftier-than-average bathroom scale. When not dispensing good or bad news, it folds up and into the wall (like a miniature version of the Murphy idea shown on page 14). Not only does the bathroom floor remain free of underfoot obstacles, but the scale stays protected, too. Design: Judy Aptekar.

A Very Private Library

Racks to display your current collection
of periodicals and paperbacks

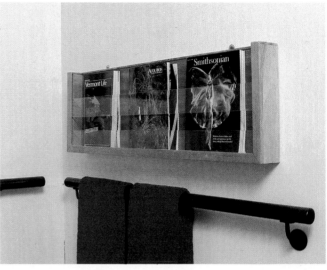

Three-in-one wall unit

With a small bathroom, you can't afford to waste even the awkward space between the toilet and the adjacent wall. The handy redwood unit shown here offers a lot in a limited area: a shallow yet roomy cabinet for extra soap and paper products, a tissue holder, and a very simple magazine rack. (Magazines stand on top of the supply cabinet and are held in place by two redwood trim strips.) Design: Marshall Design-Built.

See-through strips let magazine covers brighten bath

In this wall rack, magazines are held in place by two strips, as in the rack shown on the left. But instead of redwood, the strips here are made of clear acrylic to give a sleek, contemporary look—and to let colorful magazine covers show through. The rest of the unit is simply a shallow, three-sided wooden box. Design: John Matthias.

Cabinet creates a paperback perch

Spanning a toilet alcove, the top of this wooden medicine cabinet is home to a collection of paperback books. Open shelves are an appealing—though often overlooked—option for bathroom storage; pages 62–63 show several other ways in which creative homeowners and designers have put them to work. Design: The Butt Joint.

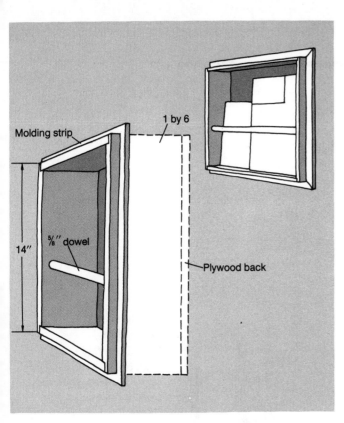

Molding strip
1 by 6
14"
5/8" dowel
Plywood back

Between-the-studs box library

This recessed rack for reading matter is a simple box that fits snugly between two wall studs. Since wall studs are usually 16 or 24 inches apart (center to center), your box library will probably need to be 14½ or 22½ inches wide; 14 inches is a convenient height for it. Locate the studs, measure and mark your wall carefully, then remove only enough wallboard to accommodate the box. (Pick a location for your box library where you won't run into electrical wiring and plumbing lines inside the wall.)

Use fir 1 by 4s or 1 by 6s for the box frame (1 by 6s will add extra depth, but they'll stick out slightly from the wall). Before assembling the frame drill shallow holes in the side pieces to hold a ⅝-inch dowel (see illustration). Assemble the frame and add a ¼-inch plywood back. Slide the unit into the wall cutout, and side-nail the box to one or both wall studs. Add molding strips or wood trim around the box to hide the rough edges and give a built-in look. Finally, finish the unit with enamel, varnish, or polyurethane. Design: John Schmid.

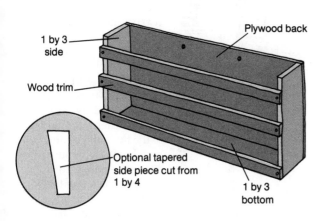

1 by 3 side
Plywood back
Wood trim
Optional tapered side piece cut from 1 by 4
1 by 3 bottom

No-frills wall rack

This simple wall rack is remarkably easy to build. Cut two side pieces and a bottom piece from pine or fir 1 by 3s, and cut a back from ¼-inch or ⅜-inch plywood. Assemble the rack, then nail ¼-inch-thick strips of wood trim across the front to keep magazines and books in place. Finally, drive two woodscrews through the back of the rack and into the wall studs and apply a paint, varnish, or polyurethane finish. The unit illustrated is approximately 12 inches high and 20 inches wide, but these dimensions can be adjusted to suit your needs and wall space.

If you must get fancy, build the rack with tapered side pieces (cut from 1 by 4s) so your reading matter tilts forward for easier access.

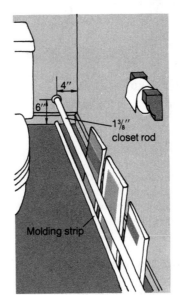

4"
6"
1⅜" closet rod
Molding strip

Closet rod corrals magazines

A 1⅜-inch wooden closet rod, mounted 4 inches out from the wall and 6 inches above the floor, can keep magazines rounded up in what would otherwise be wasted space. A molding strip attached to the floor (as shown) will keep magazines from sliding forward. If your bathroom floor tends to collect water, add a narrow wooden platform (with the molding strip on top) to keep your reading matter high and dry.

Towel Hang-ups

A whole raft of racks, rails, rods, and rings
that you can buy or build

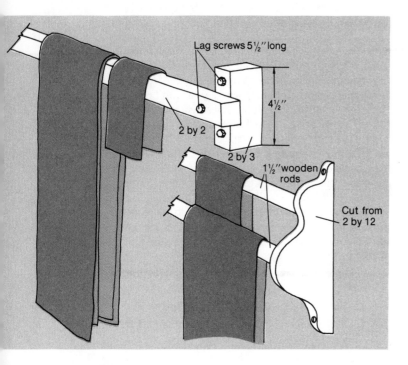

Lag screws 5½" long

4½"

2 by 2

2 by 3

1½" wooden rods

Cut from 2 by 12

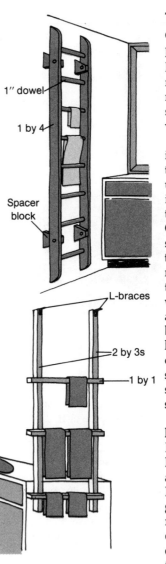

1" dowel

1 by 4

Spacer block

L-braces

2 by 3s

1 by 1

Redwood & towels—two ways to go

Here's a pair of easy-to-make variations on the basic
towel bar theme. One is a no-nonsense rail; the other is
a fancier, and slightly more challenging, two-rung rack.

The rustic rail is made from a long redwood 2 by 2
held out from the wall by 4½-inch-long end blocks
made of 2 by 3s. Lag screws 5½ inches long attach the
rail to the end blocks—and the end blocks to the wall
studs. (Be sure to find the wall studs before you decide
on a length for your rail.) If lag screw heads seem too
rustic, you can countersink them and cover them with
dowel plugs.

For the two-rung rack, use 1½-inch wooden rods and
redwood, fir, or pine 2 by 12s. From the 2 by 12s, cut two
curved wall mounts like the one shown; smooth them
with a rasp and sandpaper. Drill shallow holes in the
mounts to support the rods, positioning the lower rod in
front of the upper one, as shown. Two screws fasten each
mount to the wall studs. (Again, determine the length
of your rack after you've located the wall studs.)

A bathroom's humid climate can be tough on unfin-
ished wood, so be sure to protect your new towel bars
with several coats of polyurethane finish or penetrating
resin.

The lowdown on ladders

Floor-to-ceiling towel
ladders make the most of
narrow spaces while they
make a bold decorating
statement. They're also
very easy to build.

Recess 1-inch dowels
into matching holes in
two parallel 1 by 4
uprights; glue the dowels
in place and clamp
them securely until dry.
Or simply nail 1 by 1
strips to the front edges of
two parallel 2 by 3 up-
rights. Fasten your ladder
to the floor and ceiling
with L-braces (be sure to
allow at least ¼ inch
between the top of the
ladder and the ceiling for
clearance), or attach it to
spacer blocks that you've
screwed into the wall
studs.

Redwood is an excel-
lent material for towel
ladders because of its
handsome appearance
and moisture resistance.
Hardwoods are also
good, but somewhat
more expensive. Which-
ever material you
choose, be sure to pro-
tect it with a polyure-
thane finish or penetrat-
ing resin.

Trellis treatment

What makes this attractive towel rack a gift from the garden? It's actually a redwood trellis that has been carefully sanded to remove any splinters, then varnished for moisture resistance and screwed to the wall studs. Hooks were added for towels, accessories, and small electrical appliances.

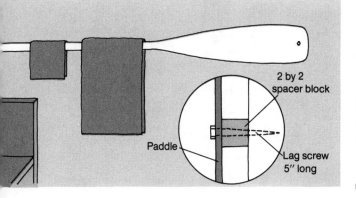

This paddle stays high & dry

This sleek 5-foot towel bar is actually a canoe paddle that was purchased for under $10 at a marine supply store. It's attached to the wall studs with two 5-inch-long lag screws that run through holes drilled in the paddle and in two spacer blocks cut from a 2 by 2. Several coats of clear marine varnish make this unusual towel bar "weatherproof."

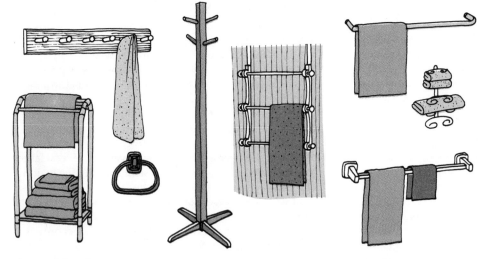

Ready-made racks

If you'd rather buy a towel rack than build one, you'll find a large selection of ready-mades. Standard bars and rings, sold individually or as components in matching accessory sets, are available in a wide variety of materials—from brass to chrome, from oak to plastic. If you have floor space to spare, consider a freestanding rack, such as a towel tree or a floor stand with room for both hanging and folded towels. Other options include wall racks with brass hooks or wooden pegs, and handy over-the-door organizers.

Small Appliance Storage

Here are several solutions to the problem of where to stash
your burgeoning collection of grooming gadgets

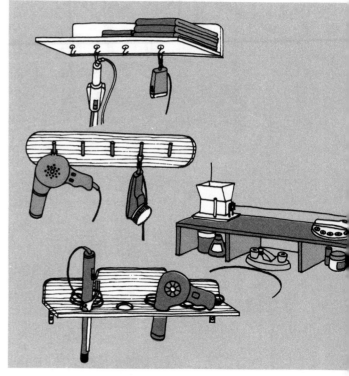

Ready-made solutions
to appliance storage problems

The popularity and proliferation of personal-grooming
gadgets have put bathroom storage at an even greater
premium. We have electric toothbrushes and water jets;
blow dryers, curling irons, and electric rollers; shavers,
tweezers, complexion brushes, and manicure machines—
but how can we keep them all organized and within
reach?

A clear acrylic appliance caddy is an attractive, though
fairly limited, solution. Designed to sit on a countertop or hang on a wall, it has a large holster for a blow
dryer and side compartments for other small appliances
and grooming aids.

Storage aids not designed specifically for small appliances can be easily pressed into service: consider shower
caddies (remember that they can be hung on an open
wall as well as over a shower head), wall-mounted vinyl
pouches (often sold as closet organizers), and under-
shelf baskets of vinyl-coated wire.

Perhaps the most flexible approach to small appliance
storage is a vinyl-coated-wire grid system. Appliances
with hanging loops can be suspended on hooks; those
without loops can be stored in the bins and baskets that
are available as components of such systems.

Some improvised solutions

If your small grooming appliances have hanging loops,
then simple hooks or pegs are all you'll need for storage.
Put together a taproom rack from a redwood backing
strip and some brass hooks or hardwood-dowel pegs; or
simply screw cuphooks to the underside of a bathroom
shelf.

If you'd rather not hang your appliances, consider a
narrow shelf with carefully measured holes drilled
through it to form holsters for your curling iron, your
shaver, or the nozzle of your blow dryer. For several large
or heavy appliances, try a wider shelf running the length
of the sink counter and 6 to 8 inches above it; support the
shelf with wood blocks spaced to form counter-level
cubbyholes for cosmetics and grooming aids. For moisture protection, finish wood shelves with enamel or two
coats of.clear polyurethane.

A pair of in-the-wall cabinets

These two recessed cabinets feature built-in electrical outlets and space for several personal-grooming appliances. The cabinet on the left is recessed into an open wall and can be camouflaged with wallpaper or paint. A mirror mounted on the inside of the cabinet door allows one-stop grooming.

The cabinet on the right makes use of the space between the medicine chest and the countertop below. Its mirrored door extends the look of the medicine chest mirror; a piano hinge and two lid supports allow it to swing down 90 degrees to form a handy counter.

Hidden door catches—magnetic for the mirrored cabinet, a touch-latch for the camouflaged one—add sleekness to both storage units. Plastic laminate keeps the inside of the cabinets bright-looking and easy to clean.

Countertop hideaway

A cabinet right on the counter can be a convenient place for the grooming gadgets you use daily. Here, an electric shaver and a dental water jet fit inside a plywood-frame cabinet that was tiled to match the bathroom counter. The appliances swing out on a hinged plywood shelf, ready for use. Cords run through a hole in the counter and down to an outlet in the cabinet below. Design: Larry Meyer.

Bath Accessories

These handy holders can give your bath a brand-new look

For a custom look— a coordinated collection

Changing accessories is an easy and inexpensive way to update your bath. Coordinated lines usually include towel racks, bathroom tissue holders, facial tissue dispensers, soap dishes, toothbrush holders, and sometimes even medicine cabinets and magazine racks. Matching non-storage items, such as electrical outlet covers and drawer pulls, are sometimes offered, too. Available in a variety of styles and price ranges, coordinated accessories are appearing now in materials such as pine, oak, plastic, brass, and chrome—as well as the popular ceramics.

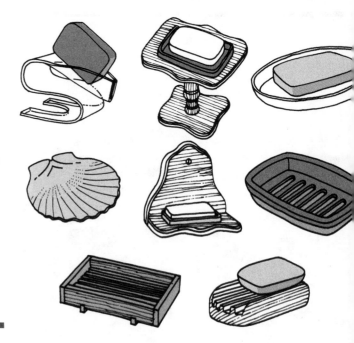

Distinctive dish designs

Soap dishes come in styles, materials, and colors to suit every bathroom decor. There are standard countertop dishes, pedestal models, and wall-mounted units; materials include ceramics, clear acrylics, glass, plastic, and the popular clear-finished woods. Most dish designs include holes or slats to facilitate drainage and save soap; or you can add one of the ribbed or spiked plastic inserts that are designed especially for this purpose.

If made-for-the-bathroom soap dishes don't appeal to you, consider using a pretty porcelain dish—or a beautiful seashell—instead.

Ceramic holder

High-tech plastic holder

Brass holders

Spring-loaded insert

Ship's-rail holder

Cut from 2 by 6

1″ dowel

Horizontal-dowel holder

1¼″ dowel

Vertical-dowel holder

Tissue holders to buy or build

Tissue holders are available in a wide variety of styles and materials—from traditional steel or ceramic holders with spring-loaded inserts, to high-tech plastic models in bright colors, to costly antique reproductions in solid brass. But tissue holders are also very easy to make, and the handsome wooden ones shown here are fine examples.

The two ends of a teak ship's rail (from a marine supply store) make a very stylish holder. Just drill a small hole in the inside edge of each piece to accommodate a spring-loaded insert (available at most hardware stores), and add shims, if necessary, to increase wall clearance. (Remember that a new roll of tissue is about 5 inches in diameter, so the insert's center must be at least 2¾ inches from the wall.)

The horizontal-dowel holder substitutes a 1-inch dowel for the spring-loaded insert. Cut two end pieces (in any shape you like) from a fir 2 by 6. Then drill a 1-inch-diameter hole halfway through one end piece and a corresponding hole completely through the other end piece (so the dowel can be removed). Allow at least 4½ inches clearance between end pieces (that's the width of a standard roll).

With the vertical-dowel holder, the tissue roll stands on end. Use scrap blocks of fir, oak, or redwood and a 5-inch-long 1¼-inch dowel. Assemble the pieces (as shown) with woodscrews and glue.

Mounting tissue holders may require some patience. Some end pieces are easier to mount if they are first bridged by a backing piece which is then attached directly to the wall. Try to anchor a holder to a wall stud; if that's not feasible, use expanding anchors or toggle bolts.

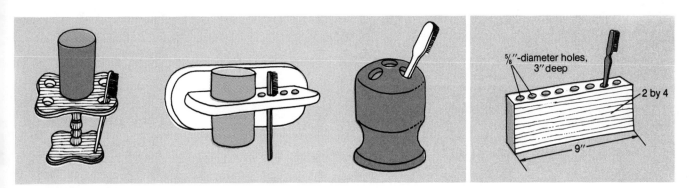

⅝″-diameter holes, 3″ deep

2 by 4

9″

Dental details: a brush-up course

Choose one of the many commercially available toothbrush holders—freestanding or wall-mounted, with tumbler or without—or make one of your own from a scrap block of oak.

Begin with a 9-inch-long 2 by 4. Into one edge, drill eight ⅝-inch-diameter holes, each 3 inches deep (see illustration). Smooth the entire holder with fine sandpaper. Finish the wood with two coats of clear polyurethane to protect it from the humid bathroom climate—and from dripping toothbrushes.

Index

Photographers

Richard Fish: 21 top. **Jack McDowell:** 10, 11 bottom, 12, 15, 18, 19 bottom, 20, 21 bottom, 22 bottom, 23 bottom, 35 bottom, 37 bottom, 39, 42, 44, 45, 46, 47 bottom, 57 bottom, 59 bottom, 62, 63 top left and bottom, 64, 65 bottom, 66 right, 69 top, 71 bottom, 72 top right. **Steve W. Marley:** 9 bottom, 11 top, 13, 14, 19 top, 36, 38, 43 bottom, 47 top, 58, 59 top, 60, 61 bottom, 63 top right, 65 top, 67, 68, 69 bottom, 70, 72 top left and bottom. **Rob Super:** 22 top, 24, 34 bottom, 41 bottom. **Tom Wyatt:** 9 top, 16, 17, 23 top, 33, 34 top, 35 top, 37 top, 40, 41 top, 43 top, 48, 57 top, 61 top, 66 left, 71 top.